Masterpieces

'A very powerful evening of theatre . . . Miss Daniels has established herself as a distinct voice with real theatrical flair.'
Michael Coveney, *Financial Times*

'Ultimately powerful and deeply disturbing . . . I came out overwhelmed by the sincerity of Sarah Daniels' writing in her play *Masterpieces*, a play which finally adds up to the most persuasive argument I've heard for banning pornography.'
Manchester Evening News

'The play has bite, anger and tenacity and many of its arguments are true . . . the supreme merit of Ms Daniels' combative work is that it makes me want to argue back.'
Michael Billington, *Guardian*

Masterpieces was first staged at the Royal Exchange Theatre Manchester, before transferring to the Royal Court Theatre, London, in 1983.

Sarah Daniels' plays include *Ripen Our Darkness* (Royal Court Theatre Upstairs, London, 1981); *Ma's Flesh Is Grass* (Crucible Studio Theatre, Sheffield, 1981); *The Devil's Gateway* (Royal Court Theatre Upstairs, London, 1983); *Masterpieces* (Manchester Royal Exchange, 1983; Royal Court Theatre, London, 1983/4); *Neaptide*, winner of the 1982 George Devine Award (Cottesloe, National Theatre, London, 1986); *Byrthrite* (Royal Court Theatre, London, 1986); *The Gut Girls* (Albany Empire, Deptford, 1988) and *Beside Herself* (Royal Court Theatre, London, 1990).

SARAH DANIELS

Masterpieces

METHUEN DRAMA

A METHUEN MODERN PLAY

First published in 1984 in the Royal Court Writers Series as a
Methuen Paperback original by Methuen London Ltd in association
with the Royal Court Theatre, Sloane Square, London SW1.
Reprinted 1984, 1985

This revised edition published in the Methuen Modern Plays
Series in 1986 by Methuen London Ltd.

Reprinted, in this newly revised edition, in 1991 by Methuen
Drama, Michelin House, 81 Fulham Road, London SW3 6RB
and distributed in the United States of America by HEB Inc.,
361 Hanover Street, Portsmouth, New Hampshire, 03801.
Reprinted 1992

Printed and bound in Great Britain
by Cox & Wyman Ltd, Cardiff Road, Reading

ISBN 0–413–41260–1

A CIP catalogue record for this book is available
from the British Library

*The photograph on the front cover shows Kathryn Pogson as
Rowena and Bernard Strother as Trevor in the 1983 Royal Court
production. From the production, the photograph on the back
cover shows Kathryn Pogson, Patti Love as Hilary and Shirley
Dixon as Jennifer. Both photographs are by John Hayens.*

CAUTION
This play is fully protected by copyright. All rights are reserved
and all enquiries concerning the rights for professional or amateur
stage productions should be made to Judy Daish Associates,
83 Eastbourne Mews, London W2 6LQ (professional) and Samuel
French Ltd, 52 Fitzroy Street, London W1P 6JR (amateur).
No performance may be given unless a licence has been obtained.

Acknowledgement
I am indebted to Dusty Rhodes for seeing the film and letting me use her description of it, as published in the *Revolutionary and Radical Feminist Newsletter*, Autumn 1982, Common Ground Community Print Shop, Sheffield.

S.D.

Snuff

Snuff is a film which first appeared in the States in 1976, so called because the actresses were actually mutilated and murdered in front of the camera – 'snuffed out'. Many 'snuff' films have been made since then. Early in 1982 it was announced that the original *Snuff* film was being distributed in this country. Feminists protested immediately and the distributors withdrew the film but not before several hundred copies had been made. Women in Leeds' 'Women Against Violence Against Women' group found several shops advertising and hiring *Snuff*. We protested. Members of the Leeds licensing committee and other councillors were asked to see the film. Many did, most walked out unable to watch the mutilation and murder scene. They demanded that it should be destroyed. A group of women from WAVAW and local press and television also saw the film. We were numbed with shock. This murder was done for the pleasure of men. The Marquis de Sade, the 'honoured' pornographer, said, 'There's not a woman on earth who'd ever had cause to complain of my services if I'd been sure of being able to kill her afterwards.'

Dusty Rhodes (*December 1983*)

Masterpieces was first performed at the Royal Exchange Theatre, Manchester, on 31 May 1983, with the following cast:

ROWENA	Kathryn Pogson
YVONNE	} Patti Love
HILARY	
JENNIFER	
POLICEWOMAN	
JUDGE	} Shirley Dixon
IRENE WADE	
TREVOR, *Rowena's husband*	} Gerard Murphy
PSYCHIATRIST	
RON, *Yvonne's husband*	
MAN IN STREET	
MAN IN TUBE STATION	} Eamon Boland
PROSECUTOR	
CLIVE, *Jennifer's husband*	
PROLOGUE, *the Baron, the Peddler, the Consumer*	
POLICEMAN	
TEACHER	} William Hoyland
MAN IN TUBE STATION	
JUDGE	

Voice overs recorded by members of the Company

Directed by Jules Wright
Designed by Di Seymour
Lighting by Nigel Walker
Sound by Chris Coxhead

This production subsequently transferred to the Royal Court Theatre Upstairs on 7 October 1983, with the following change of cast:

TREVOR	} Bernard Strother
PSYCHIATRIST	

Directed by Jules Wright
Scenery by David Roger
Costumes by Di Seymour
Lighting by Nigel Walker
Sound by Patrick Bridgeman and Chris Coxhead

Masterpieces moved into the Royal Court's main auditorium on 5 January 1984.

Masterpieces is set in London. The events take place over twelve months in 1982 and 1983, and shift back and forth throughout the year.

Scene One

A restaurant. JENNIFER *and* RON, *and* TREVOR *and* ROWENA *are dancing.* YVONNE *sits at the table. Male monologue in three parts: all played by the actor who plays* CLIVE.

The sound of Concorde landing. The dancers freeze. Light on the BARON.

1. When I was at university, my one aim in life was to go into business and get rich quick. I was extremely ambitious and not about to wait around for middle-aged spread to set in before I made it. My enterprise, enthusiasm and hard work paid off. In the last few years the tax man has gleaned over two million pounds from me. I have always kept on the right side of the law and when I was first called a purveyor or filth, it upset my mother a lot, but ours is a perfectly normal profession run by ordinary nice people, not gangsters or kinky dwarfs in soiled raincoats. That is a ludicrous myth perpetuated by the media.

   We do sometimes lose stock in police raids, but we allow for the costs when building our stocks so, sadly, the consumer ends up paying more than he should.

   Profit margins are high. Our trade makes more money than the film and record business put together. It will be the growth industry of the eighties. Just as betting shops were in the sixties and casinos in the seventies. I sincerely believe, had it not been for the present repressive climate, I'd have received the Queen's Award for Industry long ago. My mother? Well, she soon stopped crying when I bought her a luxury house in the country.

   The dance continues, then freezes. Light on the PEDDLER.

2. I suppose it was about ten, no twelve years ago when the market for naughty underwear and sex aids really opened up. Funnily enough I was working in a newsagents when this mate of mine told me there was a vacancy in one of what is now a large, established chain of shops and he could fix it for me. Well, I jumped at the chance and being the manager of a sex, I mean, private shop, I'm never stuck for something to say at parties even if it doesn't go down too well with the wife, know what I mean? The vast majority of our custom comprises normal healthy men. (*Slight pause.*) Oh, and women, that's why our shops have carpets on the floor, women like that, makes them feel at home. We have an in-joke about getting our underfelt. But seriously though, we've gone to great expense to get an easy atmosphere. It's just like wandering around a boutique. Of course we'll always have criticism from the frustrated politicians and their pathetic fanaticism for censorship. Hopefully, though, the majority of the population is liberated enough to wake up to the fact that we sell marital aids which enrich people's — men and women's — romantic lives, that we provide the practical side to sex therapy.

The PEDDLER *exits.* ROWENA *and* TREVOR *sit. Enter* CLIVE, *the* CONSUMER.

3. Oh, I suppose it depends what you mean by pornography. Yes, I buy magazines, sometimes videos. It's not something clear cut or mechanical, sex I mean. Everyone has fantasies, don't they? And from time to time they need revising or stimulating, otherwise like everything else it gets boring. It's simply a question of whatever turns you on. Let's face it, alcohol and cigarettes can kill people, looking at pictures never hurt anyone.

CLIVE *takes his place at the table.*
JENNIFER *and* RON *walk to the table and sit down.* RON *has been telling her a joke which has amused her. She is relieved, however, to be out of his grasp.*

TREVOR (*to* JENNIFER). I see he's kept you amused.

JENNIFER. Entranced.

RON (*to* TREVOR). We were chatting about holidays. Have you two made any plans this year?

TREVOR. We've sort of mutually agreed we can't afford it.

ROWENA. Might have a week in Cornwall.

RON. Package tour. Often works out just as cheaply if not cheaper.

CLIVE. That's what I keep telling Jennifer.

JENNIFER. Darling, I am not going on a package tour. As a breed, the British abroad are foul.

RON. At least you can usually guarantee a good dose of currant bun.

JENNIFER. They should all be shot.

RON. Pardon?

CLIVE. She is referring to her fellow-countrymen. We spent Christmas in Morocco last year. Never been the same since, have you darling?

RON. Apparently the food out there is horrible.

JENNIFER. The food is divine – so is the country. Only, for the rest of the crowd we went with, it might as well have been Margate. Do you remember all those hideous coach tours? – just like one of those office beano affairs.

ROWENA. Mother, don't be such a snob.

JENNIFER. God, you must be joking. Who can afford to spend a fortnight in Morocco at Christmas? This was the privileged élite.

CLIVE. At least you got your precious suntan. And enough juicy titbits to dine out on for the rest of the year.

JENNIFER. Yes, do you remember that day . . .

CLIVE. Not now, you've done it to death.

ROWENA. How come Mum always has the monopoly on funny stories?

CLIVE. Your mother has a warped imagination.

JENNIFER. He means because I'm a joke.

CLIVE (*through clenched teeth*). I did not mean that at all, darling.

RON. We heard a good joke in the pub, the other lunchtime. Do you remember, Trev?

TREVOR. I doubt it, I can never remember jokes.

ROWENA. Bad as me, darling.

RON. I wouldn't say that.

ROWENA. At telling jokes, Ron.

RON. Oh that's it, hang on. Two nuns walking through a forest, right? When a man jumps out on them and rapes them, one of them reckons, 'How are we going to explain to the Mother Superior that we've been raped twice?' The other one says, 'But, Sister, we've only been raped once.' 'I know,' says the first, 'but aren't we going back the same way?'

The men laugh, TREVOR *not as heartily as the other two.* ROWENA *rather hesitantly joins in.* YVONNE *doesn't even smile, while* JENNIFER *laughs uproariously and rather disconcertingly so.*

CLIVE. The only one I know is about the nun who was raped but she didn't mind because he was a saint. 'How do you know?' asked the other nuns. 'Because he had Saint Michael on his underpants.'

Same response only they don't find it as funny except JENNIFER *who laughs even louder.*

TREVOR. That's as old as the hills.

RON. What was the other one?

TREVOR. I don't know.

RON. Yes you do, I heard you tell it to Frank.

TREVOR. Oh.(*He is rather abashed.*) 'Help, I've been raped by an idiot.' 'How do you know?' 'Because I had to tell him what to do.'

There is the same pattern of response.
JENNIFER *laughs raucously.* YVONNE *remains silent but extremely uncomfortable, wishing she could just walk out.*

RON. What's your idea of an ideal date? She screws until four o'clock in the morning, then turns into a pizza.

Response is as for the first joke.

JENNIFER. I know a good one.

CLIVE. My dear, I don't think so.

RON. Come on, Clive.

CLIVE. You haven't heard my wife's jokes.

JENNIFER. Don't spoil it, there's a dear. Now there was this vicar and the headmistress asked him to give a talk to the fifth year.

CLIVE. Get on with it, darling.

JENNIFER. Do you mind?

CLIVE. Well you're hamming it up.

JENNIFER. How?

CLIVE. Fifth year, first year, second year, what does it matter? It's of no relevance.

TREVOR. Let her get on with it, Clive.

JENNIFER. Thank you, Trevor.

CLIVE. You've not heard the end yet.

JENNIFER. He won't live to hear the end if you don't stop interjecting.

CLIVE. You're dragging it out.

JENNIFER. Now you've got that out of your system may I proceed?

CLIVE. All right, if you think you must.

JENNIFER. Seconds away round two.

CLIVE (*to the others*). See what I mean?

JENNIFER. There was this vicar.

CLIVE. We know, we know. You've said that once.

JENNIFER. You've ruined the flow, so I'm going to have to start all over again.

RON. Let her get on with it.

JENNIFER. There was this vicar who was asked to give a talk about sex to the fifth year of a school in his parish. However, when he came to writing the appointment in his desk diary he didn't want to write sex as his wife might find it.

RON (*trying to be funny*). Find what?

JENNIFER (*grimaces*). His diary. So he wrote talk, at such and such a school, on sailing. The time came to give the talk and it was received very well. A couple of weeks later his wife met the headmistress in Sainsbury's and the headmistress said, 'Your husband gave a wonderful talk to our fifth year,' and the wife replied, 'I don't know how, he's only done it twice. The first time he was sick and the second time his hat came off.'

Although the men laugh they are less inclined to do so.
YVONNE *smiles.*

ROWENA. Mother, trust you.

JENNIFER. Just wanted to prove I could hold my own.

CLIVE (*flatly*). Very adequately too, darling.

ROWENA. You're a bit quiet, Yvonne.

YVONNE. Well I . . .

TREVOR. Probably hasn't been allowed to get a word in edgeways all evening.

ROWENA. Don't look at me. I haven't been holding forth about woofers, tweeters, wattage and speakers all evening.

RON (*puts his hand over* YVONNE's). Still waters run deep.

JENNIFER. How sweet.

CLIVE. I'm seriously thinking of investing in a Bang & Olufsen.

ROWENA. Oh no, don't start Trevor off. He'll be green with envy.

JENNIFER (*to* CLIVE). What a shame you can't seriously think of an investment in tiling the bathroom.

YVONNE. How many men does it take to tile a bathroom? (*Pause.*) Three but you have to slice them thinly.

TREVOR. Couldn't you see your way clear to investing in one for me, Clive?

JENNIFER. I don't think tiles are the 'in' thing for stripped pine bathrooms.

ROWENA. I think he meant the hi-fi system. He's been on about getting a better one ever since I can remember — just a little boy's fantasy.

JENNIFER. I wonder what Freud would make of that.

ROWENA. Who cares?

CLIVE. Surely a social worker can't dismiss him out of hand?

ROWENA (*unsure*). Well . . . no . . .

CLIVE. He hit the spot in lots of ways.

YVONNE. Crap! Who's ever wanted a penis? What woman has ever wanted a penis?

JENNIFER *laughs genuinely*.

Have you ever wanted one, Row?

ROWENA. Er, yes, well, I wasn't defending him, very outdated ideas, ha. You were saying you weren't enjoying teaching much these days.

YVONNE. Actually Ron said that.

RON. Well, it's true, isn't it?

TREVOR. Row's pretty fed up with her job, aren't you?

ROWENA. Sort of. (*To* YVONNE:) D'you remember when we were at school, I said if it were the last choice on earth I wouldn't be a social worker and you said you'd rather clean toilets than teach?

YVONNE (*smiles*). Yes, high ideals of youth.

TREVOR. I suppose some goddess or other with her lack of

control over the inequality of the sexes drew you into the nurturing professions, synonymous with the feminine role.

ROWENA. You can laugh.

JENNIFER. It must be very messy trying to shove the working classes into inappropriate institutions when they clearly don't want to go.

ROWENA. I can assure you I'm not like that, Mother.

JENNIFER. I'm sure you're not. I meant the concept as a whole.

CLIVE. You're as adept at analysing social work as you are at telling jokes.

JENNIFER. Am I? How sad. I thought my jokes were really rather funny. (*To* YVONNE:) Do you teach secondary age, dear?

YVONNE. Yes.

RON. She hates it, don't you, love? It's the discipline especially.

YVONNE. I'd like to get out of teaching altogether.

ROWENA. What would you do?

YVONNE. I quite like the idea of proofreading. You know, sitting in an attic all day correcting manuscripts.

TREVOR. Or womanscripts as the case may be.

RON. All those squiggly hooks and things would drive you round the bend.

ROWENA. I don't think I'd like it much myself.

JENNIFER. Oh, it sounds quite appealing.

CLIVE. You would think that.

JENNIFER. Would I?

CLIVE. You're halfway there — round the bend I mean.

JENNIFER (*forced smile*). Oh, don't be mean, darling.

CLIVE (*forced smile*). Only joking, darling.

ROWENA. Is it all the preparatory work that's getting you down?

YVONNE (*clearly doesn't want to talk about it*). Yes, yes, everything.

RON. Come on, Yvonne. It's not that. You've always enjoyed teaching. It's the boys, isn't it?

YVONNE. Ron.

RON (*wants to explain his wife's unsociable behaviour*). I don't know if you're acquainted with adolescents today, but controlling them is damn near impossible.

ROWENA. I can imagine. I have nightmares about a couple of lads on my case load, but *en masse* I think I'd freak out.

TREVOR. Oh yeah? You've got a couple of headcases, but put you in front of a class of nubile sixteen-year-old boys and they'd have trouble controlling you.

JENNIFER. Ah ha, my daughter has another side to her.

ROWENA (*lightly*). Trev, please, not in front of the parents.

RON. It's all these girlie mags they bring in, playing on your nerves, aren't they, love?

ROWENA. Nothing's changed, they used to snigger at them in the cloakroom when we were at school.

JENNIFER. Same here, only in our day a nude ankle was enough to raise a snigger.

RON. I wondered what you were going to say then.

JENNIFER. Now, now, don't encourage me.

CLIVE (*to* JENNIFER). Darling, speak for yourself. I am not Victorian, I assure you, it takes more than an ankle . . .

JENNIFER. Thank you, Clive.

YVONNE. It's much more open and explicit now.

TREVOR. Is that necessarily a bad thing?

YVONNE. When a boy holds up a picture in front of the class and says, 'She's got more up top than you, miss', or 'Can you do this, miss?', yes it is.

TREVOR. I can see that it would provide a distraction from Gerard Manley Hopkins.

YVONNE. I teach history.

TREVOR. Or even King Lud and the Luddites.

ROWENA. What do you do?

YVONNE. What can I do? If I had my way I'd burn the lot of it.

TREVOR. Oh hang on, that's really rightwing.

YVONNE. Is it?

ROWENA. I've never thought about it much. I suppose if women want to do it and men want to look at it, where's the harm?

RON. I keep telling her most men look at it, and the more upset she gets the more the lads will play up.

ROWENA. Do they? (*Silence.*) Do you ever look at it, Trevor?

TREVOR. No, but I have seen it, some of the blokes at work leave it lying around.

ROWENA. You never told me.

TREVOR. I didn't tell you we had a digital thermometer or an electronic pencil sharpener either. So what?

ROWENA. And do you have any true-life confessions, Clive?

CLIVE. Is nothing sacred between stepfather and stepdaughter?

JENNIFER (*cheerfully*). Don't be modest, darling, you've got a video cassette library which could put the BFI out of business.

CLIVE. Oh films, I thought you meant filthy magazines.

JENNIFER. *Playboy* and *Mayfair* in the lav.

CLIVE. Oh, and you read the interviews in those, but I would never look at the really hard stuff. God, I couldn't bear the idea of children and animals used like that.

JENNIFER. I suppose it depends what you mean by pornography.

YVONNE. All of it, everything from adverts to . . .

RON. Love, it's totally innocuous.

TREVOR. I've got nothing against it. Just wish I had a low enough IQ to enjoy it.

ROWENA. Maybe it does have a positive side. To enable

inadequate men to act out their fantasies, save them from
attacking anyone on the street.

YVONNE. Does social work for the child-batterer consist of
showing them pictures of parents torturing their children,
with the children appearing to enjoy it — as a preventative
measure?

ROWENA (*unsure*). No.

TREVOR. Come on, there's absolutely nothing to connect it with
violence.

YVONNE. It is violence, violence against women.

RON. All right, darling. Thank you.

YVONNE. I didn't mean to bore you.

JENNIFER. I'm glad you did. (*The* MEN *laugh.*) I mean, not
bore us, not that you did but . . . What do the men on the
staff think?

YVONNE. They don't give a damn. Even the local chip shop
keeps a pile of magazines for the boys to browse through
at lunchtimes.

CLIVE. Business is business.

YVONNE. It's a bloody conspiracy.

RON (*lightly*). Now love, don't act paranoid, especially in front
of a social worker.

YVONNE. And who does the complaining about broken lights
in corridors and lifts on estates? Is it a coincidence that they're
all women or are they all paranoid?

TREVOR. What is it they say — 'Just because you think you're
paranoid doesn't mean they're not all out to get you' or
something?

ROWENA. It's very difficult for both sexes, boys have a lot of
pressure on them to perform, you know.

YVONNE. Aren't we lucky to be living in a liberal society, next
it'll be poor little Hitler, wasn't he a victim of epilepsy?

ROWENA. You can't be so one-sided, Yvonne.

YVONNE. Crimes committed against women have never been credible, why change now?

RON. Amen. Yes, my love, we don't want to put Lord Longford out of a job, do we?

JENNIFER. Very stimulating thought. Oh, Clive, darling, you've gone very quiet.

CLIVE. I was contemplating getting my cheque book out. You know how that sends me into a frenzy of silence.

RON. Yes, time to make a move.

JENNIFER. Oh dear, I was just starting to enjoy myself. My main problem at the moment is . . .

CLIVE. Not now, darling. Your daughter specialises in problems all day long.

ROWENA. Unfortunately there is very little variation, unemployment or unemployment.

RON. Hey, that's what I meant to say to you, Row. There's a job going at my place. Just photocopying and stuff. If anyone you know can fill it — it's theirs.

ROWENA. Thanks, I'll bear it in mind.

RON. A nice girl though please, no troublemakers, punks or glue-sniffers.

ROWENA (*slight edge*). Even 'nice' people can't get work these days, Ron.

JENNIFER. It must be so boring for the poor devils.

CLIVE. You should know. The last time you worked, Noah was still painting the ark.

JENNIFER. With money life can be irksome, without it it must be tediously boring.

CLIVE. Irksome?

JENNIFER. Well, apart from my horticultural cohorts, of course.

CLIVE. Oh God . . . the damn women's flower arranging guild.

JENNIFER. We are far from damned, Clive darling, thank you.

TREVOR. What does it entail?

JENNIFER. Wondrous things, my boy. Not suitable for your delicate earholes.

RON. Does that apply to me as well?

CLIVE. Don't start her off.

JENNIFER. It's quite jolly really. We infiltrate exhibitions with our outrageous arrangements.

RON. A line in suggestive cacti?

JENNIFER. Oh no. Mine was a lovely dried number set in an oasis and for the base I used my diaphragm.

ROWENA. Mother, really.

JENNIFER. I have no use for it. It seemed a shame to think it was totally obsolete. And then Madeline grew mustard and cress in an empty pill packet.

CLIVE (*flatly*). Yes, very funny.

JENNIFER. Of course, not half as funny as your misogynist jokes.

CLIVE. Misogynist? Me?

JENNIFER. And then someone else grew these delightful little cultures — like ferns — on a sanitary towel.

The men look embarrassed. YVONNE *laughs.*

ROWENA. What on earth for? Why?

JENNIFER. Boredom. Everyone else is so stuffy. When we reached the change of life you know, menopause — we all decided we were perfectly entitled to act mad. We took a collective decision to be mad, as you might say.

CLIVE (*mutters*). I can't see how a decision actually came into it.

JENNIFER. On the contrary, it was a very intellectual discussion. We decided to get our revenge on society for writing us off. Mind you, we're running out of ideas.

ROWENA. If you're not careful you'll find yourself planting a daisy in the buttonhole of a man in a white coat.

JENNIFER. Ah, what does the future hold for your batty mother? What will I be doing in a year's time?

CLIVE. Don't tempt me.

JENNIFER. I often wonder, if I had a way of looking into the future, whether I'd bother.

YVONNE. I know I wouldn't dare.

TREVOR. See some terrible event and spend the time in between dreading it.

ROWENA. You're so pessimistic, Trevor, this time next year I reckon I'll have got promotion and you'll have your Bang & Olufsen.

CLIVE (*looks at his watch*). Unless we make a move, you won't be fit for work tomorrow, let alone next year.

CLIVE, JENNIFER, RON *and* TREVOR *go off.*

The sounds of a courtroom. ROWENA *moves to her court position.* YVONNE *watches her, then speaks directly to the audience.*

YVONNE. Rowena has this standing joke with me. Something along the lines of me being acutely aware of oppression from the day one of my brothers threw a copy of *Biggles Flys West* at me in my cot. Tch, that's a gross exaggeration. In fact, I can't remember seeing a book in our house. It was against considerable odds that I got to grammar school, let alone college. Not that it didn't cost a lot of teasing, both at home and down our street, and not that it taught me a lot either . . . a different way of thinking . . . a different set of values. (*Pause.*) But I was twenty-six before I learnt that the words 'I feel' and 'I think' were neither synonymous nor interchangeable . . . and there's no way I read that in any book.

The endless hours I've spent rejecting and rebelling against my mum and her catatonic, cast-iron clichéd philosophy of life, only to find a sort of grim truth in the wretched phrase — 'There's only one way to learn things — the hard way.'

Actually it was when I went away to college that I met

Ron at a party. He was working for his dad at the time in a mini-cab firm and there was something I really liked about him. Looking back, I think it was his MG sports car.

Exit YVONNE.

Scene Two

A crown court. ROWENA, JUDGE (*a woman*), POLICEMAN.

CLERK (*voice over*). All stand.

JUDGE. Rowena Stone, you are charged with the murder of Charles Williams. How do you plead — (*Silence.*) guilty or not guilty?

ROWENA. Neither.

JUDGE. Mrs Stone, as I'm sure you are well aware, this court does not have a procedure for neither. Are you guilty or not guilty?

Silence.

ROWENA. Not guilty.

JUDGE. Officer, would you be good enough to describe the events to the court in a little more detail?

POLICEMAN (*reading from a notebook*). On the seventeenth of this month I was proceeding in a westerly direction along Seven Sisters Road, when I noticed a commotion outside Finsbury Park Tube and the Inspector, I mean the ticket inspector . . .

JUDGE. Constable, just the events if you please, not a blow by blow account of your diary, otherwise you won't have anything new to say when you're cross-examined, will you now?

POLICEMAN. Madam.(*He attempts to précis his notes by reading faster.*) Anyway, when I got to the platform, I noticed a man, who was later identified as Mr Charles Williams, deceased, under the 10.15 p.m. from Walthamstow to Brixton tube train. An eyewitness who is prepared to testify to the fact said,

'She pushed him', whereupon I cautioned and questioned the accused who remained silent.

JUDGE. Did anything strike you as odd, constable?

POLICEMAN. Madam? (*He tries to think of something which might be construed as odd.*) Well, now you mention it, the tube driver kept jumping around shouting, 'Not another one, how many more bloody suicides am I going to get?' Obviously he wasn't fully aware of the situation and I think he was in a state of shock.

JUDGE. We are not assembled here to uncover the vagaries of your thought processes, constable.

POLICEMAN. We are trained in shock treatment, madam.

JUDGE. I meant anything peculiar in the manner of the accused?

POLICEMAN. Oh no, madam, she was as cool as a cucumber.

JUDGE (*to* ROWENA). Is this true?

ROWENA. No, I was in a state of shock.

JUDGE (*impatient*). Is the description accurate?

ROWENA. For the most part.

JUDGE. Specifically.

ROWENA. I believe it is impossible to proceed in a westerly direction along Seven Sisters Road, but the rest is true.

JUDGE. Mrs Stone, are you now changing your plea to guilty?

ROWENA. No.

JUDGE. I understand you have no defence lawyer.

ROWENA. Correct.

JUDGE. Mrs Stone, I propose to adjourn. To allow you time to reconsider your decision not to be represented and to give you time for legal aid to be arranged. Psychiatric reports will undoubtedly be called for.

ROWENA. Do you think I'm mad?

JUDGE. Fortunately, I do not have unlimited power. I am not in a position to label the sane insane or vice versa. I do

feel obliged to say, however, how distressed I am to see you
in front of me now, as I have always found your attitude
to the law, in your professional capacity as a social worker,
most sensitive and coherent.

ROWENA. Pity the same may not be said for the law's attitude
to me.

JUDGE. Adjourned.

CLERK (*voice over*). All stand.

Scene Three

Playground sounds.
 A classroom. YVONNE, *after school, sits there alone marking
books. Voices off are those of a male teacher. Enter* IRENE
WADE.

IRENE (*timid*). Mrs Hughes?

YVONNE (*looks up abruptly*). Mrs Wade.

TEACHER (*off*). Rogers, haven't you got a home to go to? Then
I suggest you go. Now. Pronto.

IRENE. I hope you don't mind me coming to see you like this.

YVONNE. Is your husband with you?

IRENE. No, I came on my own. He doesn't know.

YVONNE (*relieved*). Oh, I see. (*Then:*) I really don't see how I
can help you.

TEACHER (*off*). Gregory, get out of there and stay out.

IRENE. I've been very down lately, especially after I went to
see Ian on Saturday.

YVONNE. Mrs Wade, you are talking to the wrong person.
I was responsible for your son's conviction. If it hadn't
been for me the whole matter would have been dropped.

IRENE. It's just . . . I don't know.

YVONNE (*abruptly*). You think he's been punished too severely?

IRENE. Well, I don't know.

YVONNE. Mrs Wade . . .

IRENE. Irene, please . . .

TEACHER (*off*). What are you lads doing skulking about the cloakroom area? I don't care, you shouldn't be here. Vanish.

YVONNE. Mrs . . . Irene . . . perhaps you should talk with the headmaster, you'd get a more sympathetic response.

IRENE. I know, he says the same as the lawyer. She'd only been raped but was unharmed.

YVONNE. I for one am not about to shout about how lucky she is, not today, or ever. If it hadn't been for me, no one would have bothered even to talk to her.

IRENE. Where is she?

YVONNE. She had to get a transfer. As though she hadn't been through enough and . . .

TEACHER (*off*). No, you can't go back and get it. It will have to wait until the morning.

YVONNE. And the worst of it is your son has been made a cult hero.

IRENE. If it had been my daughter I'd have wanted him hung from the nearest tree, but I don't . . .

TEACHER (*off*). Jamison, you disgusting brute, get out of here and report to the headmaster first thing in the morning. I can't find anything to laugh at. And that includes the rest of you as well.

YVONNE. Where were we?

IRENE. I wouldn't have your job for the world.

YVONNE. I'm sorry, some days I feel sort of schizophrenic, a cross between Joyce Grenfell and Attila the Hun.

IRENE. I understand. I won't take up any more of your time, Mrs Hughes.

YVONNE. No wait, Irene. I have no sympathy for your son. None. Not that I don't have any for you, but I do understand

if you feel it amounts to one and the same thing. (*Pause*.)
And my name's Yvonne.

TEACHER (*off*). This is the last time, clear off home!

IRENE. I . . . I just don't know what to say, or do, or anything.
I feel I could have stood by him over anything else . . . I'd
rather he'd done anything else.

YVONNE (*softer*). You feel he needs your support?

IRENE. He had all my support before. I don't know what I did
or didn't do wrong. I might make all the same mistakes again.
All those psychiatrists spent more time with me than they did
with him. Where did I go wrong?

YVONNE. You mustn't blame yourself.

TEACHER (*off*). I will not tell you again, Lawrence.

IRENE. Why not? Why on earth not? Everyone else is.

YVONNE. Nobody in their right mind — which doesn't
necessarily include the medical profession — is blaming you.
I'm certainly not.

IRENE. Yes they are. They all are. A normal healthy boy rapes
a girl. Was I too prudish? Too open? Too domineering? Too
weak? Too much of a nag? Did I discourage him too violently
from playing with his genitals as a baby? Did I sit him too
viciously on the potty? Did I smother him? Did I neglect him?

YVONNE. For what it's worth, I know it's not your fault.

IRENE. When I used to read of those things in the paper, I used to
say castration was too good for them.

   Long pause.

   Can you tell me what I do with the love for my son?

YVONNE (*pause*). I'm sorry, I don't know.

IRENE. Perhaps you know what to do with this. (*She gives her
a carrier bag stuffed with magazines*.)

YVONNE (*pulls one out and looks at its cover*). But these go
back to seventy-eight.

IRENE. I always made it a rule that children should have privacy,

but now he's away I thought, well, it would be wrong not
to clean his room out — mind, they were well hidden. I
suppose that was wrong as well.

YVONNE. You and your husband had no idea?

IRENE. I supposed all young boys looked at it. As for my
husband, ha, it never bothered him.

YVONNE. You think your husband encouraged him?

IRENE. Didn't have to. He has a drawerful of his own. Only
difference is, he doesn't have to hide it.

A MALE TEACHER *enters, crosses to the window and bangs
his fist on it.*

TEACHER. Rogers, I told you to go home hours ago. Now get.
(*To* YVONNE *and* IRENE:) Sorry.

Scene Four

HILARY's *flat. She is ironing.*
The day after the meal, ROWENA *has some evening visits,
one of whom is* HILARY PETERS. ROWENA *is trying to be
bright and breezy without appearing to be trying too hard.*

ROWENA. Hello, I'm from the Social Services, can I come in?

HILARY. If yer must.

ROWENA (*following* HILARY). My name's Rowena, can I call
you Hilary?

HILARY. If that's what turns yer on. I s'pose you'll be
wanting a cup of coffee.

ROWENA. No thanks, I've just had one.

HILARY. Not stopping long, then?

ROWENA. Are you busy?

HILARY. As a matter of fact I'm up to me eyes with the *Sun*
bingo. I know the Social money ain't s'pose to go on luxuries

like the daily papers but then I'm a deviant, but of course you
know that anyway.

ROWENA *tries to laugh casually*.

HILARY. Forgot me manners. Sit down. Won't you please?

ROWENA (*sits down*). Thanks. (*She tries to take in the
surroundings subtly*.)

HILARY. Well, what d'yer want?

ROWENA. Nothing. Nothing special. I just called round to see if
everything was all right.

HILARY. I might be thick but I know there's no such thing as
door to door social work, not with this government anyway.

ROWENA. Okay, your previous social worker phoned me.

HILARY. Oh Gawd, the late Mrs Crawley.

ROWENA. She's not dead.

HILARY. More's the pity. No, I always used to call her the
late Mrs Crawley on account of she was always late. Trouble
with you lot, you read too deeply into things what aren't
there.

ROWENA. Oh I see, and she asked me to pop in and see how
you were getting along.

HILARY. And here I was thinking, one good thing about getting
me transfer was getting you nosey bleeders off me back.
(*Pause*.) No offence like.

ROWENA. It's just that I thought I'd introduce myself so that if
you ever did need anything you'd know where to come.

HILARY. Ta.

ROWENA. You've got a little boy, is that right?

HILARY. What of it? You can't take him away you know, I look
after him proper, he don't go without nothing.

ROWENA. I can assure you I have no intention of doing any
such thing. What's his name?

HILARY. Heathcliffe.

ROWENA (*thinks this is a breakthrough*). Emily Brontë?

HILARY. Na, Kate Bush.

ROWENA. Who?

HILARY. The record, you know (*She sings.*) 'Heathcliffe it's me, it's Cathy —'

ROWENA. Oh. (*Then:*) My mum was reading *Ivanhoe* when she was pregnant with me. That's where I got my name.

HILARY. I don't blame you for changing it. Rowena's strange enough but Ivanhoe — God what a mouthful.

ROWENA. No, Rowena's a character in it.

HILARY (*flatly*). Oh, really.

ROWENA (*casually*). Do you still maintain contact with the father?

HILARY. S'no point.

ROWENA. Maintenance.

HILARY. You're joking. They'd only take it off me. The DHSS. Then after a couple of months he'd stop paying and I'd have to take him to court. No way.

ROWENA. Does he still see Heathcliffe?

HILARY. No.

ROWENA. Where is he?

HILARY. Dunno.

ROWENA. Heathcliffe?

HILARY (*sarcastic*). Oh dear me, now where did I leave him? Out playing on the window ledge? Or was it the M11? (*Then:*) He's down his Nan's.

ROWENA. That's nice, does she live close by?

HILARY. As it happens.

ROWENA. Is there anything you're concerned about that I might be of any help with?

HILARY. Money.

ROWENA. Well, as you know we have no means of offering long-term financial support.

HILARY. You have no means of offering nothing. What d'you do, eh? All the people you see, the only thing what's wrong with their lives is money and all your fancy ideas and posh words can't cover up nothing. At the end of the bleedin' day the only advice you can give us is to march in and say (*She assumes a German accent.*) 'You vill learn to budget.'

Long pause.

Right, look sorry. I didn't mean to go on at yer — you ain't halfway as near as bad as the last one. Thatcher had nothing on her, I reckon her facepacks was made of chainmail.

ROWENA. We've had some complaints from the neighbours.

HILARY. I see, now you want to prove you can't be manipulated. Yeah, big word for me ain't it?

ROWENA. About men, drunk on the landing at all hours.

HILARY. Don't exaggerate.

ROWENA. It's not true then?

HILARY. I've got men friends, yeah. But then if I had female friends you'd reckon I was the other way and have my boy in care quick as a flash.

ROWENA. Hilary, I do not have the power to whip children into care unless there is proof that they're being maltreated.

HILARY. And then you whip 'em, in care, eh?

ROWENA. You know what I mean.

HILARY. I ain't never so much as laid one finger on him and I keep him looking real smart. Yeah, I know I look like something the Oxfam shop rejected but I always keep him smart. He has everything new . . . Nothing secondhand. Do you know how much a pair of kid's shoes cost?

ROWENA. And your boyfriends help you out? (*Pause.*) There must be better (*She corrects herself.*) easier ways of clothing Heathcliffe.

HILARY. Oh right. Hit me with 'em.

ROWENA. I know employment's hard to find.

HILARY. And I ain't exactly got golden bonuses either — no qualifications — on me own — a kid.

ROWENA. What did you do before he was born?

HILARY. I ain't never had a job then neither.

ROWENA. How old are you?

HILARY. Look at it on the bright side — I've only got another thirty-six years before I retire.

ROWENA. You've never worked?

HILARY. Not unless you count my CSE needlework project. You're s'posed to be a social worker. Where you bin?

ROWENA. Sorry.

HILARY. What for? Ain't your fault.

ROWENA. Do you enjoy, er, doing it?

HILARY. Do me a favour.

ROWENA. Why? Then, I mean, why do you do, er, it?

HILARY. They reckon we're all sitting on a gold mine, don't they?

ROWENA. That lucrative?

HILARY. Even I ain't heard of that one.

ROWENA. That much money in it?

HILARY. No, for me there ain't, no.

ROWENA. If you had a job would that be OK?

HILARY. What you going to do, give me yours?

ROWENA. I'm just thinking . . .

HILARY. Yeah, but who'd look after Heathcliffe? Me mum can't, not all day.

ROWENA. If we got him a place in a day nursery.

HILARY (*weary*). He's been on the waiting list since he was born.

ROWENA. If we could . . .

HILARY. And if a pig orbited the moon.

ROWENA. Is that what you want?

HILARY. What . . . a bacon satellite? Do you think I want to live like this? Course I want a job.

ROWENA. I can't promise but I'll do my best.

HILARY (*not nastily*). You sound like Mrs Crawley. She was a girl guide captain in her spare time. D'you really not want a coffee? S'no trouble.

ROWENA. Thanks. (*She looks at her watch.*) But I've got two other visits this evening.

HILARY. Blimey. You work unsociable hours.

ROWENA (*smiles*). Me?

HILARY. And I don't even get no sick pay neither. Honest, I want a job. I really do.

ROWENA. To want a job is hardly to be in the minority, to have one is.

HILARY. Do what?

ROWENA. Do you mind what work, er, which work. I mean the work you do — within reason?

HILARY. I'll take anything what'll give me enough money to live on — with proper wages packet and National Insurance.

ROWENA. I'll be in touch.

Scene Five

10 p.m. ROWENA is walking home after her last visit. A MAN walks behind her. (This is quite 'innocent'. There is no threat of attack.) ROWENA and the MAN freeze, then walk again.

ROWENA (*voice over*). Wish I wasn't wearing a skirt. I look quite respectable though. What am I doing out this late at night? Working. The only women who work at night are prostitutes. Otherwise their husbands would meet them. Don't walk fast, it will look funny. Don't slow up — inviting. Don't look too nervous. Why the hell doesn't he cross over?

They pass each other. They look back.

ROWENA's *living-room.*

TREVOR (*grabs her*). Boo! Got yer.

ROWENA (*jumps out of shock*). Get away from me. What the hell are you doing?

TREVOR. What's the matter? Jesus Christ.

ROWENA. Don't do that.

TREVOR. Do what?

ROWENA. Jump on me, you stupid sod.

TREVOR. Thanks a bunch, I was only taking the trouble to welcome my wife home from a hard day at the office.

ROWENA. Well don't.

TREVOR. Bloody hell. At least I don't loll in front of the telly demanding my dinner.

ROWENA. Just go around scaring the bloody life out of me.

TREVOR. No need to bite my head off just because you're late.

ROWENA (*sits in a chair*). Everything took longer than I expected.

TREVOR. Pity you don't get overtime, you'd be worth a fortune.

ROWENA. All right. I've earned an afternoon off in lieu. No, spare me the toilet jokes.

TREVOR. I was going to say, you're looking rather flushed.

ROWENA (*groans*). Dreadful. How was your day?

TREVOR. Boring. Except Harriet's house burnt down, that's why she was off.

ROWENA. Oh no, poor woman.

TREVOR. Yes, even I felt a bit sorry for her.

ROWENA. Was anyone hurt?

TREVOR. No, only the dog – burnt alive, but that appeared to be an ill wind anyway. Because, next door apparently had taken legal action against it because it had had a fight with their terrier and killed it. I ask you. How could you take a dog to court? What would it say when it got there? Alec reckons it would take a bow wow. Anyway that's hypothetical as it kicked the bucket Joan of Arc style.

ROWENA. Where is she now?

TREVOR. In the little doggie paradise. No, I s'pose after what it did the doggie hell.

ROWENA. No, fool, Harriet.

TREVOR. With relatives. (*Joking.*) You're home now, you're s'posed to switch the caring off.

ROWENA. You haven't got a job going have you?

TREVOR. You can't be that fed up.

ROWENA. Not for me, nana, that young woman I told you about who we thought was on the game, well she wants to get off.

TREVOR. Hey Row, you can't jump in all shining morality. If that's what she's chosen to do.

ROWENA. Choice. That seems rather an inappropriate word.

TREVOR. Perhaps it's your particular values that are inappropriate.

ROWENA. Since when has wanting a job become a middle-class value?

TREVOR. When you choose to overlook the fact that by other definitions, she's a working girl.

ROWENA. She said she wanted a proper job. She doesn't like what she does.

TREVOR. Of course she said that to you. What do you think she was going to say — a screw a day keeps the tax man away.

ROWENA. I think she meant it.

TREVOR. Pull the other one. (*Then:*) You know they've been

wanting to tax it for years — just haven't found a way — short of inventing accountants to accumulate sperm returns.

ROWENA. Trevor.

TREVOR. Sperm is a perfectly respectable term.

ROWENA. Well that's it, then. Ron.

TREVOR. Interesting word association.

ROWENA. I'll give him a ring a bit later on.

TREVOR. I should have thought that dinner party was enough social intercourse to last a lifetime.

ROWENA. Stupid combination, Mum, them and Clive.

TREVOR. Your mother's one thing, but Yvonne, she's something else.

ROWENA. Poor Yvonne, we used to have such a laugh at school. I can't believe the change in her.

TREVOR. You say that every time we see them. If she laughed now the shock would kill her.

ROWENA. Mind you, it can't be easy being married to a man who pretends to be a reincarnation of Jack the Lad.

TREVOR. What do you mean by that?

ROWENA. Those banal jokes.

TREVOR. Honestly, sometimes you can be so snotty. Okay, so they weren't that funny, but couldn't you see he felt out of his depth, and with that bourgeois bitch who passes herself off as my mother-in-law it's hardly surprising.

ROWENA (*hurt*). Trev.

TREVOR (*defensive*). Well, she can't stand me.

ROWENA. That's purely projectionist. You can't stand her.

TREVOR. I know what projectionist means. She's cracked, round the bend, nutty, potty, and if she'd been one of your clients you'd have had her in the funny farm by now. But no, because of her breeding, nobody would dare slap a loony label on her. She's quite at liberty to pass as eccentric.

ROWENA. She's still my mum.

TREVOR. Yeah, well, sorry, it's just that, well, it was a perfectly enjoyable meal until Yvonne suddenly found her tongue, and then the atmosphere, well, we might as well have been in a fall-out shelter.

ROWENA. Maybe she had a point, she's unhappy.

TREVOR. There are ways and ways of making a point and a tirade from a friend's wife at a dinner party with one's in-laws present does not go down a bomb.

ROWENA. I thought you didn't care about your in-laws. Make up your mind. Besides which she's my friend, and your friend is her husband.

TREVOR. Don't let's bicker. I should count myself lucky I'm not your friend's husband. There for the grace of God etcetera.

ROWENA. She's very bright, you know.

TREVOR. I didn't say she wasn't. She made one or two intelligent remarks underneath the neurosis, but God, the way they were put across was so fanatical. Proofreader? How could she sit down and objectively proofread a Leslie Thomas novel? No wonder their sex life is a disaster.

ROWENA. Remember that stuff we were talking about?

TREVOR. What stuff?

ROWENA. Those magazines, could you bring some home?

TREVOR. What for?

ROWENA. Never looked at any before. Never know, it might improve my night life.

TREVOR. That and a Terylene duvet.

ROWENA. I thought my heavy breathing turned you on.

TREVOR. I've managed to distinguish the sighs of ecstasy from the intermittent asthma attacks. Spoilt it a bit.

ROWENA. What do you mean, their sex life is disastrous? How do you know?

TREVOR. What a scatty mind. That was about twelve sentences ago.

ROWENA. Well?

TREVOR. Ron told me one lunchtime in the pub.

ROWENA. Oh, do you often discuss your sex lives then? And what do you say about me, Don Juan? 'Trouble is, Ron old chap, nudge, nudge, snigger, snigger, I can't tell if she's actually orgasmed or if it's her allergy to the feather duvet.'

TREVOR. Of course not. It just spilled out one day. No wonder he's fed up.

ROWENA. Couldn't possibly be his fault though. Oh no.

TREVOR. For God's sake, Row, anyway I can't bring that stuff home.

ROWENA. Why?

TREVOR. Well, they'll think, I don't know what they'd think, but it would look funny.

ROWENA. Okay then.

TREVOR. It's just stupid. Tell you what, I'll buy you a copy of *Playgirl* instead.

ROWENA. Thanks, oh master.

TREVOR. Don't mention it, my darling.

ROWENA. Are you using the car tomorrow?

TREVOR (*teasing*). Might be.

ROWENA. Oh go on, let me. Can I, please? Clever Trevor.

TREVOR. Might let yer.

ROWENA. Go on. (*She kisses him.*)

TREVOR. For you, anything.

Scene Six

RON *and* YVONNE *at home.* YVONNE *is reading.*

RON. Right little ray of sunshine.

YVONNE. So you have repeatedly told me.

RON. Life and soul of the party.

YVONNE. Let's drop it, shall we?

RON. When it suits you, yeah, we drop it, but then you start opening your trap in public.

YVONNE. I didn't bring it up, Ron, you did.

RON. If only by way of your bloody poface.

YVONNE. I don't see what good it will do dragging it up again.

She continues to read.

RON. Oh don't you? No, but you don't see any point to communicating with your husband at all. Well that's the last we'll see of them in a long time. You know that silly cow Rowena can't stand you.

YVONNE. Can't she?

RON. Why do you think you've not heard from her?

YVONNE. Well, er, I'd not thought about it.

RON. Because, take it from me, she only sees you out of courtesy.

YVONNE. She's not the sort.

RON. When was the last time she phoned? Eh?

YVONNE. We've been friends for ages.

RON. You're an embarrassment, God, you're so involved with yourself, you can't see how stupid she thinks you are.

YVONNE. She's the only friend I've got.

RON. Is that surprising? I mean, ask yourself. You want to listen to yourself, constant moan, moan, moan. Small wonder you have no friends. (*Knocks the book from her hands.*) You don't even try, do you? You can't even be bothered to talk to me. Do I really repulse you that much?

YVONNE (*picks up the book again*). I'm not very happy.

RON. You're not happy? Christ, what d'you think I am? Over the moon, eh? Over the bloody moon. My God, my wife won't even speak to me, barely lets me come near her. Jesus Christ, Yvonne.

YVONNE. Please, Ron, not now.

RON (*mimicking her*). Not now, not now, darling. I've got a headache. A bad knee, athlete's foot, ringworm, tapeworm, aversion to sperm.

YVONNE. I can't take any more.

RON. You can't take any more? That's rich, you spoilt bitch. I wish they'd said something on the marriage contract. After five years your wife will be fucking frigid.

YVONNE. Ron, the neighbours.

RON. The neighbours, the poxy bloody neighbours. We have to listen to their squeaking bedsprings half the night. I'm sure they won't mind listening to the explanation of why they can't hear ours. I'm sure it'll be a relief to one and all. (*To the wall:*) Won't it?

YVONNE. Shut up.

RON. Typical. Anything you don't want to hear, like the truth, gets shut off. Shut out and shut up. Yvonne, you are married to me!

YVONNE. I'd noticed.

RON. Well, I can't say I had, not lately anyway.

YVONNE. What do you expect, eh? (*She screams.*) Shout at me all day, then expect me to make mad passionate love to you at bedtime?

RON. Don't give me that. I've tried every tack. Short of hanging myself, nothing but nothing I could do would please you.

The phone rings. Pause. Neither of them is about to answer it then RON *picks it up.*

RON (*sharply*). Hello. (*Then nicely:*) Oh hello, Rowena. (*To* YVONNE:) It's for you. (*He shoves the receiver towards her.*)

YVONNE (*taking the receiver*). Hello Row. (*Pause.*) Oh, fine, fine. Yes, right. Here you are. (*She hands the phone back to* RON.) She wants to speak to you.

RON (*to phone*). Sorry, I automatically assumed . . . (*Pause.*)
Yes, yes. It's still vacant. How old is she? Fine, yes, that'll
be okay, as long as she's not a terrorist, ha ha. (*Pause.*)
Oh thanks very much. Great. Give us a ring then. Bye.

YVONNE. What was that about?

RON. She wanted to speak to me not you.

YVONNE. About the job?

RON. Amongst other things. She didn't have much to say to you.

YVONNE. Not a lot.

RON. She obviously prefers to talk to me.

YVONNE. Only to ask you a favour. Still, perhaps I should go
round and apologise.

RON. She reckons she'll invite us over to dinner, so I wouldn't
bother. (*He sits next to* YVONNE *who tries not to tense.*)
Don't worry, you can patch it up. Can we though?

YVONNE. Ron.

RON (*coaxing*). Come on, what's happened? Am I really that
bad, eh? What's the matter? What's happened to us?

YVONNE. You think it's all my fault.

RON. I said 'we' didn't I? (*He strokes her hair.*) Let's forget it,
mmm.

YVONNE. Umm.

RON. Coming to bed?

YVONNE. In a minute.

RON. Don't be long. (*He gets up and kisses the top of her
head.*) You know I love you.

He goes out.

YVONNE (*hands over face, quietly*). I hate you.

Scene Seven.

HILARY. *Monologue.*

HILARY. When I was young, what am I saying? I mean when I was about thirteen I used to look at the boys in our class looking at us, and think how odd that they wanted to stick their cocks in us. Straight up, I did. Seemed such a peculiar thing. Anyhow, then I learnt it was natural and didn't think no more about it. Our school joined the grammar school that year and we was then comprehensive so all that meant was the grammar school lot done O levels and we, if we was really lucky, done CSEs. Also it meant like in the eyes of the boys that them lot were prudes and we was slags. I never figured out which ones were best to be in but I reckoned, looking back, we had the most laughs.

I told the social worker I ain't never had no qualifications but the truth of the matter is that's rubbish. I ain't entirely up shit creek 'cos I also got a CSE Grade 1 in Needlework — comes in handy sew to speak, ha ha. I weren't much interested in anything else. Nothing else on the timetable that is, but I tell you I could've got an A level, a Ph.D. even, in contraceptives. It weren't no fault of me own I fell for me kid.

Me and me mate Shirl had it sussed, we read everything we could lay our hands on. Having bin stuck with the label 'slag' it seemed stupid not to live up to it. But, as Shirl remarked at the time, if they only knew we aren't so much nympho-maniacs but contraceptomaniacs. I lost me virginity when I was nearly fifteen. I bunked off school. His parents were at work, not that it was a case of one thing led to another. No way. It was planned to the last letter — French letter. But them things are unreliable — the machine in the King's Head pub got 'British Made' on it — some cleverdick had written underneath, 'So was the *Titanic*'. So I made him get some of that Delfen foam stuff as well. I still think how brave he was going into the chemist to ask for it — but he must have thought it was worth it. What does I do though? Puts the applicator in the top of the bottle shaking on account of me nerves and the whole thing spurts all over the wall. Anyhow, we done it after we'd wiped it off. I don't know what I was expecting. (*She shrugs. Pause.*) He kept his socks on.

It was all getting a bit traumatised 'cos I don't know if you've ever had it off up the back of Ilford Pallie, but with foam, applicator and packet of three to contend with you sort of lose track of why you wanted to do it in the first place, know what I mean?

Anyhow, when me and Shirl was sixteen we decided enough was enough, and took ourselves off to the Family Planning. That was a real laugh only we was scared stiff at the time. We shuffled into the waiting room and grabbed a magazine and started to read it casual like. It was Shirl who had the nerve to look out, well, I don't know if it was nerve or whether there weren't much in the *Horse and Hound* what interested her. Anyhow we needn't have worried 'cos all you could see was pairs of hands clutching magazines, not a face in sight.

Then, oh my God, then we had this talk about all the different contraceptives. Me and Shirl reckoned we'd like to do that job, after all, that's what we spent all day talking about. Mind you, we started giggling like mad 'cos on this like card table with a green felt top was everything in the way of contraceptive wear you could imagine, looking really decrepit, 'cos they was only for show. The funniest thing was this pink plaster model of your insides like, you know, that picture in the Tampax instructions. Only having never seen a cross-section of me insides it was difficult to make out what was what — the fact that it was chipped to buggery didn't help matters none.

Anyway, they did our blood pressure but the weighing machine was broke, so they had to guess that, and then all these questions. I don't think they believed I was sixteen. Giggling in their faces couldn't have helped matters much. And then I had to have an internal. Can't tell you how much I'd been dreading it. There was some delay while I tried to figure out if I'd had sex in the last three days. 'Because of the sperm count my dear.' Then I said what did it matter 'cos we used a Johnnie anyway. They looked gobsmacked. I tell yer gobsmacked, like, 'Oh she might have an IQ after all.'

What they thought of me, I'm amazed they never sterilised me on the spot. I told 'em, I did, straight. I said, 'If I'd been doing it all this time with nothing I wouldn't be here. I'd be up the maternity ward, my dear.' I tell you I was so nervous when they told me to slip me lower garments off I took me socks off an' all. Then this plastic bag on a hand looms towards me treading on me clothes in the process, I might add. Shirl, lucky beggar, got out of it by telling them she was on, she wasn't but she's always one step ahead that girl.

Still it was easier, being on the Pill, like. Though didn't make much difference, more messy in another sort of way, if you know what I mean. I remember the name of it: Minilyn. I thought if I ever get a little house with roses round the door I'd call it Minilyn. Still at sixteen I was old enough to know me life had been mapped out. Not that I wasn't grateful to get this flat, I bloody was and it's really nice inside now.

So how did I get up the club? Well, Shirl cocked things up of her own accord, 'cos, like I told you, she never took no notice of what anyone else said. She figured out if you started to take one packet straight after another you didn't have to worry about the week of the month when he didn't want it. So of course they found out and thought it was 'cos she was thick and took her off of it. So then she had one of those loop things, God, who would credit a little bit of wire with causing so much pain. There was times when she fainted, but one thing about Shirl, she weren't no coward. And as it turns out it wrecked her insides. She had it taken out last year and they reckoned she was probably infertile, tried to blame it on her getting VD or something — it weren't true. It had fucked her insides more than any Hampton Wick had done.

But they took me off it eventually 'cos of me blood pressure and I had to make an appointment for a cap fitting. Shirl made some stupid joke about inside leg measurements but I weren't having one of those coil things. Anyhow, I missed the appointment on account of me Nan's funeral. I remember thinking in the dust to dust bit, yeah and me from foam and rubber back to . . . yeah well — the bloke I was with didn't like going back to Johnnies much neither, that funny rubber smell really lingers on yer fingers. I discovered this stuff called 'C' Film. You have to insert it if you're a woman and he has to fit it on his whatsername like a handkerchief on a head but then I finds out that it's not effective until after an hour. S'ats okay fer a woman but have you ever known a bloke keep it up for an hour?

So what happens — round the back of the multi-storey car park one day and we'd only got one Durex — I taken to persuading him to wear two but I thought oh well, it's a chance in a million. And if I'm ever going to write me life story that's what I think I'll call it, *A Chance in a Million* but I wasn't done for. No. I know about douching. I read somewhere that there was something in Coca Cola what kills sperm. I don't know if it's true now. I suspect they took it out when they took whatever it was out that acts with Codeine. Any rate, we runs all the way to the off-licence. And this over-helpful shop assistant tries to persuade us that a can's cheaper than a bottle but we insisted on a bottle, then we had to buy a bottle opener, didn't we? He must have thought we were nuts — come to think of it, he was right.

Anyhow I douched meself with it — it seemed to have delayed reaction, it wasn't till I got home did I suddenly feel uncomfortable when I sort of erupted like in me best beige trousers. When I missed me first period I persuaded meself it was just worry but I sat up every night and prayed to God, said I'd do anything — even join the Salvation Army — threw meself down the stairs for good measure, but I don't reckon God took much to the idea of me with a tambourine. Me mum guessed, carted me off to the doctor's, saying, 'I didn't expect anything else of yer,' but the way she created it was kinda obvious she did. The doctor was a very nice, kind, moral man who thought abortion a sin. Bumbling sod. Still, I'm glad now 'cos I love my kid. That night me mum and dad had a set-to. He was carrying on at her: 'It's all your fault, you silly cow, you should have told her about precautions — you should have known that was the last thing she'd think about.' I laughed meself all through morning sickness on that one.

Scene Eight

ROWENA *is in her garden.*
  YVONNE *enters.*

YVONNE. Row.

ROWENA. Christ, Yvonne, hello.

YVONNE. Sorry am I disturbing you?

ROWENA. No, no, come through. Trevor never does anything in this garden except mow the law.

YVONNE. It's just that I saw the car outside — and then there was no answer at the door.

ROWENA. Oh hell, you can't hear anything over this. Shall we go indoors?

YVONNE. No, no, you carry on.

ROWENA. Do you want a cup of coffee?

YVONNE. No . . .

ROWENA. Or a drink . . . ?

YVONNE. No thanks . . .

ROWENA. Or something?

YVONNE. It's okay.

  Pause.

ROWENA. Nothing wrong?

YVONNE. No, no, I'm okay, fine. Fine.

ROWENA. Good. Good.

YVONNE. I only came round for a chat.

ROWENA. That's nice.

YVONNE. Well, no, to apologise really.

ROWENA. Don't be silly.

YVONNE. Last time we met I wasn't exactly on top of the world, if you remember.

ROWENA. Don't worry. We can't all be on top form all the time.

YVONNE. Only I seem to be perpetually wingeing.

ROWENA. You're no happier then?

YVONNE. You could say that.

ROWENA. How do you mean?

YVONNE (*lightly*). Oh, you know, waking up in the morning wishing you hadn't.

ROWENA. I'm sure it's not that bad.

YVONNE. I just wish moaning was a competitive sport. I'd be a world champ.

ROWENA. A holiday maybe?

YVONNE. I'm not a client you know.

ROWENA. I'm sorry, I didn't mean it to sound like that.

YVONNE. No. (*She smiles.*) I know.

ROWENA. Did Ron tell you he's fixed one of my clients up with a job?

YVONNE (*flatly*). Wonderful.

ROWENA. She's really thrilled about it.

YVONNE. How nice of him.

ROWENA. Considering she's totally unskilled, it was.

YVONNE (*flatly*). Is she attractive?

ROWENA (*shrugs*). Yes . . . yes I suppose so.

YVONNE. That's the only qualification she needs then.

ROWENA. Oh, come on. You and I didn't get our jobs because of what we looked like.

YVONNE. We have the dubious benefit of a white man's middle-class education coupled with the fact that my husband isn't our boss.

ROWENA. Jesus, you are bitter.

YVONNE. Yes.

ROWENA. What's the matter?

YVONNE. Nothing.

ROWENA. I think the sooner you get out of that school the better.

YVONNE. And I always thought the first principle of social work was to get the clients to suss out the main problem for themselves.

ROWENA. I won't say another word.

Long pause.

YVONNE. I hate Ron.

ROWENA. Oh.

YVONNE. I hate everything about him.

ROWENA. Look, you have had a rough time lately, admittedly . . .

YVONNE. Especially sex.

ROWENA. But you can't take it all out on him. (*She pauses, awkward.*) Umm, yes well, we all go through times . . .

YVONNE. I don't hate the mechanics so much . . . I just hate Ron.

ROWENA. It's a phase.

YVONNE. Really.

ROWENA. Look, what do you want me to say? I thought it was school that was bothering you.

YVONNE. They're all mixed up together.

ROWENA. Oh Yvonne, I can't see how.

YVONNE. Men, it's all to do with the way men are taught to view women.

ROWENA. Now you've lost me.

YVONNE (*indicating her carrier bag*). Every week I seem to be confiscating this stuff at school, and as if that's not enough in itself, every week I get into trouble with the headmaster because the kids complain that it costs a lot of money.

ROWENA. Actually I wanted Trev to bring those magazines at the office home with him, but he wasn't too keen.

YVONNE. I'm not surprised.

ROWENA. Can I have a look at it?

YVONNE. Only if you think you must.

ROWENA *looks at the magazines in such a way that the audience is not exposed to their contents.*

Female monologues. (Voices over on tape)

1. I suppose it would be stupid to say I did it because I wanted to be good at something and yes, okay, it gave me money and status — status, ha bloody ha. I wasn't dragged off to do it by the hair or anything but it was a different story when I wanted out. You don't get promoted in this lark. Your value is your body, when it starts to go, you get into the rough stuff and can be threatened within inches of your life — to do the nasties with animals and that. I tell you, the animals get treated like they was the royal corgies, you get treated like dirt.

2. When I was a little girl, I was always being shown off to relatives, made to sit on uncle's knee. I learnt to flirt, was told that I was pretty and I liked the attention, I loved it. I still like my body being appreciated. When I was seven I was sexually interfered with by a male relative. I never told anyone. I'd learnt by then that I was dirty and it was my fault. I went into the business for money. I had no morals at that time, I was twenty and had a two-year-old daughter to support — sure the blokes assumed they could sleep with you whenever they wanted. I went to a meeting once where these women were talking about the links between violence and pornography. Huh, I told them it was a load of puritan bullshit. Makes me laugh now. It never occurred to me to take into consideration the abuse I'd suffered personally. All I ask is that my mother or daughter never find out.

3. You're supposed to do these pathetic antics, which would cause you permanent damage in real life, with ecstasy radiating off of your mug. Once in this game it's harder than you

would imagine to get out. And if I go for a proper job, what would I say at the interview? 'Well, the last thing I did was a split beaver shot of me strapped naked to the front of an XJ6'. I also 'starred' in a film specially made by a television company for the Falklands lads who watched the stuff to get their bloodlust up. What could I give them, poor as I am? If I were a wife or a mother I could give my man. But I have the commodity of my body, and so they took that.

ROWENA (*closes book*). I don't want to look any more.

YVONNE. I'm sorry, Row. I didn't mean . . .

Pause.

ROWENA. How they must hate us.

TREVOR *enters. Pause.* YVONNE *starts to clear magazines.*

No. Can you leave them?

YVONNE. I was going to burn them.

TREVOR. That's what the Nazis did with propaganda they didn't like.

YVONNE. I think I'd better go.

TREVOR. Goodbye.

YVONNE. See you Row.

She goes out.

ROWENA. Yes okay. (*To* TREVOR:) Did you have to be so rude?

TREVOR. Me? Bloody hell. You set me up didn't you?

ROWENA. I what?

TREVOR. Let's see Clever Trevor's face when he practically falls over the stuff. That'll be a laugh.

ROWENA. You must be joking. That's rubbish, talking of which, just look at them.

TREVOR. What sort of a wanky idea is that?

ROWENA (*picks up a magazine*). Read that bit.

TREVOR. Yes, yes . . . atrocious, very badly written. (*Slight *pause*.) Rubbish.

ROWENA. Badly written? Trevor? These things go into millions of homes.

TREVOR. So does *Crossroads*, no need to get hysterical.

ROWENA. Next you'll be telling me to keep a stiff upper lip.

TREVOR (*calmly*). Rowena, love . . .

ROWENA. Don't you 'Rowena love' me.

TREVOR (*lightly*). I've started so I'll finish. I might be able to understand if I were a real pig but don't forget I was the one who introduced you to the *Female Eunuch* — the book as opposed to Yvonne.

ROWENA (*unbelieving*). Trevor!

TREVOR. Don't I do my share of the housework, the shopping, cooking . . . ?

ROWENA. And don't you always make a big show about it. Tell me what you've done; running to me for approval.

TREVOR. Don't twist things.

ROWENA. How many things do I do that go without recognition? Do I come running to you to say, 'Oh, Trevor look what I've done. The washing, the ironing, made the bed.'?

TREVOR. I've made the bed. It consists of straightening the duvet which takes approximately one second.

ROWENA. You know what I mean.

TREVOR. I've never raped anyone. I've never so much as attacked a single woman.

ROWENA. So that makes it okay.

TREVOR. In my book I should think so . . .

ROWENA. For other men to do it . . .

TREVOR. What can I do about that?

ROWENA. You could do something . . . I don't know, write, complain, about these . . . sex shops . . .

TREVOR. Sex shops? What do you know about them? They sell

sex aids for men and women.

ROWENA (*picking up a magazine*). According to this ad they sell whips, canes, dog collars, masks, hard-core porn, inflatable life-size dolls, torsos and electric vaginas for men to masturbate into. And it must be true because there it is — the mail order form.

TREVOR. All right, all right, don't lecture me for Chrissake.

ROWENA. I want you to understand.

TREVOR. To understand? To understand what? That you want total hostility between people in the street?

ROWENA. Trev . . .

TREVOR. Well, that's what you've got in your own back garden.

TREVOR *goes out. Lights fade.*

(*Interval.*)

Scene Nine

ROWENA *with a* PSYCHIATRIST.

PSYCHIATRIST. And you claim, Mrs Jefferson-Stone, that looking at pornography was the turning-point?

ROWENA. Yes.

PSYCHIATRIST. Enough of a turning-point to make you try to kill a man?

ROWENA. Yes.

PSYCHIATRIST. Would it also be true that you became obsessed with pornographic material?

ROWENA. I became obsessed with the way women are viewed by men.

PSYCHIATRIST. How did your feelings manifest themselves at the time?

ROWENA. I became extremely angry.

PSYCHIATRIST. Even though, subjectively, you had never been exposed to or threatened by sexual assault?

ROWENA. I felt sexually assaulted every time I went out —
adverts for everything from oranges to Opels, all sold with
women's breasts.

PSYCHIATRIST. You became prudish?

ROWENA. If that means I found it unacceptable, yes, I became
prudish.

PSYCHIATRIST. Can you specify — pinpoint — what exactly
you objected to?

ROWENA. The objectification of women.

PSYCHIATRIST. If you'll forgive me for saying so, you don't
strike me as the type of woman to be fanatical about this
sort of thing.

ROWENA. What sort of women would you expect to be angry at
the way women's bodies are cut up, mutilated and violated
for entertainment value?

PSYCHIATRIST. For a start you're wearing a skirt.

ROWENA. I am fully dressed, or had that escaped your notice?

PSYCHIATRIST. In the light of the conversation, indeed, it had
not.

ROWENA (*abruptly turns her chair away, then to herself*). I have
tried . . .

PSYCHIATRIST. To do what? Murder an innocent man.

   ROWENA *roars with laughter.*

   Mrs Stone, you are becoming evasive.

ROWENA. Why? Because I'm wearing a skirt?

PSYCHIATRIST. And incongruent.

ROWENA. I must try and answer the questions a little more
articulately then. In reply to the question of my dress
which seems to fascinate you.

PSYCHIATRIST. I didn't say that.

ROWENA. I could say, I can continuously compromise my
iconoclasm with conformist clothing camouflage when

complying with the correctness demanded of ceremonies such as these.

PSYCHIATRIST. That does not give much away except perhaps an obsession with the letter 'c'.

ROWENA *laughs*.

You lost all sense of reality at this time.

ROWENA. Quite the opposite. I gained all sense of reality.

PSYCHIATRIST. You also lost your sense of humour. That's true, is it not?

ROWENA. How can it be? You've made me laugh twice.

PSYCHIATRIST. As you are quite well aware, on neither occasion was I making a joke.

ROWENA. Then maybe you're in the wrong profession.

PSYCHIATRIST. What I meant was, I am given to understand, that during the last few months you wore jeans constantly.

ROWENA. If you believe that's a symptom of madness, I'd keep quiet if I were you.

PSYCHIATRIST. And in the last six months before you left your husband, your sexual life was unsatisfactory.

ROWENA. No. We didn't do it, which was very satisfactory as far as I'm concerned.

PSYCHIATRIST. And this contributed to your feelings of inadequacy.

ROWENA. I didn't feel inadequate.

PSYCHIATRIST. Do you masturbate?

ROWENA (*thinks — 'I don't believe this'*). Do you?

PSYCHIATRIST. I believe you've been seen by various colleagues of mine.

ROWENA. Indeed I've been subjected to a psychiatric battering.

PSYCHIATRIST (*trying to look at the reports in front of him with discretion*). Tell me about your relationship with your mother.

ROWENA. Go to hell.

PSYCHIATRIST. Would you concede that your opinionated and dogmatic nature shows an insecure assertiveness?

ROWENA. Tell me, would you concede, that you are a wanker?

PSYCHIATRIST. Mrs Stone, I am not of the opinion that you are insane and were it not for the seriousness of your crime be quite prepared to put it down to the premenstrual tension, PMT factor.

ROWENA. What, for 365 days of the year? Why that is magnanimous of you.

Scene Ten

HILARY *and* RON *at work. HILARY is filing or trying to get on with some appropriate office work. RON is merely being 'friendly', i.e. he does not grope her, neither are his words loaded with lust.*

RON. How's it going, Hilary?

HILARY. Okay, thanks, Mr Hughes.

RON. Good. Enjoyed your first few weeks with us?

HILARY. Very much, thank you.

RON. I'm glad to see you like the job.

HILARY. Ta.

RON. Good, good.

Pause.

HILARY. Nothing wrong is there? I mean, I'm sorry about those invoices but it was the photocopier really.

RON. No, no, it could happen to anyone. I thought we could go for a drink at lunchtime.

HILARY. It's okay, thanks, I don't drink lunchtimes, it makes me nod off in the afternoon, know what I mean?

RON. A coke then?

HILARY. I never drink coke, ta.

RON. How about after work then?

HILARY. I've got to collect me little boy.

RON. I thought your mother did that.

HILARY. From the nursery but I have to go straight to her place of work.

RON. Well, tomorrow lunchtime it is then.

HILARY. It's really very kind but I have to do me shopping lunchtimes.

RON. Kind, nothing, I always take new members of staff to lunch. It's a tradition.

HILARY. Oh.

RON (*jokey*). No need to sound so enthusiastic.

HILARY. I'm sorry, Mr Hughes.

RON. Ron.

HILARY. Ron.

RON. Are you finding it too long a day?

HILARY. Oh no, it's great really. No, it's just right.

RON. How far do you go?

HILARY. Pardon?

RON. How far do you have to travel?

HILARY. Oh, it's easy on the tube.

RON. Where do you live again?

HILARY. Er, like I say, it's only twenty minutes on the tube.

RON. I remember now. Finsbury Park. How silly of me. I go that way most evenings. I can drop you off.

HILARY. It's very nice of you but . . .

RON. No buts . . . It's no trouble.

Scene Eleven

JENNIFER *and* CLIVE's *living-room.* CLIVE *is about to watch a video. He puts it in the recorder but doesn't get a chance to switch it on. Enter* JENNIFER.

JENNIFER. Did you buy it?

CLIVE. No, my darling, I hired it.

JENNIFER. Oh no, Clive, how many times do I have to tell you? It's a racket. Hiring of videos is just a front for those places to get your address. Now we'll get the damn thing pinched again.

CLIVE. I don't see why that should bother you.

JENNIFER. And what has my husband got to entertain himself with? (*She picks up the cassette case.*) *Violate the Bitch.* Don't you have something a little more romantic, say in French with subtitles, *Violez la biche,* so much prettier don't you think?

CLIVE. Who rattled your cage?

JENNIFER. Rattled. Me?

CLIVE. Go to bed.

JENNIFER. What makes you think I want to go to sleep?

CLIVE. When it comes to a toss up between sleep or my company with regard to entertainment potential, sleep usually wins. (*Pause.*) What's the matter?

JENNIFER. I'm bored. It's hell.

CLIVE. True.

JENNIFER. I think I was biologically determined to be bored. My first rattle probably bored me.

CLIVE. People who are bored are usually extremely boring. Why don't you sit down and watch this with me? It might rejuvenate your interest in other toys.

JENNIFER. The only movement to come out of the dying embers, darling, is the bloody death rattle.

CLIVE (*weary*). Oh, go to hell.

JENNIFER. What do you mean, go? Heavens, don't try to tell me that there's a worse existence than this. Perhaps I'd better ring the Samaritans.

CLIVE. Ring the blasted Pope for all I care, but stop opening and shutting your poisonous mouth before the verbal battering does permanent damage to my ears.

JENNIFER. Fine. When you stop martyring yourself and stop wimping about like a henpecked eunuch and stop watching this filth.

CLIVE. I have had enough.

JENNIFER. I would have thought so, yes, but in the light of your unsociable viewing hours, the odds are stacked against you. If you're henpecked, what does that make me — cocksucked?

CLIVE. Hardly.

JENNIFER (*picks up the video*). What do you have to buy all this trash for?

CLIVE. You're so narrow-minded.

JENNIFER. I bloody well am not.

CLIVE. If I'd imagined for one minute how you'd have turned out, I'd never have married you.

JENNIFER. And if I'd known you'd knock off three secretaries concurrently, maybe I'd have thought twice about marrying you.

CLIVE. At least they didn't nag.

JENNIFER. Nag? You know why the dog is considered man's best friend? Because you can hit, shout at and abuse dogs and they still come back for affection.

CLIVE. Whereas women sulk.

JENNIFER. Or worse still, kick back and commit crimes of disobedience. A nag by any other name.

CLIVE. Then I suggest you stop making yourself hoarse.

JENNIFER. Ha, ha, ha.

CLIVE. You, do you know something? You're mad, mad as

a hatter, you should have been certified years ago.

JENNIFER. Thanks a bunch. And if they'd used you as a yardstick to measure sanity by I would have been. If you're the walking, breathing model of normality, it's a compliment to be mad.

CLIVE. Jesus, I feel sorry for your first husband. It must have been the biggest relief of his life when he dropped dead.

JENNIFER. Shut up.

CLIVE. And your freaky children, God, not that I don't feel sorry for them. Having you as a mother must surely qualify them for some state benefit.

JENNIFER (*sarcastic*). Oh, but of course having you as a step-father made up for all that.

CLIVE. At least I get on far better than you ever did with your foul daughter and son-in-law.

JENNIFER. It's not her. It's him. Creep.

CLIVE. You were pleased as punch when she married him.

JENNIFER. I must have been in a trance, persuading myself that a man whose only asset was a double-barrelled name would make my daughter happy. It's a scientifically known fact that to have a brain and a double-barrelled name is a genetic impossibility.

CLIVE. At least they've dropped the other name and the hyphen.

JENNIFER. I haven't heard from her since then.

CLIVE (*sarcastic*). Oh dear, that's come as a big shock.

JENNIFER. I wonder if anything's wrong.

CLIVE. What could possibly be wrong? The discovery that beanshoot and lentil quiche gives you cancer? She can't stuff another green pepper because it's ideologically unsound to penetrate vegetables.

JENNIFER. Frankly, you couldn't stick your prick into a green pepper properly.

CLIVE. My dear, a green pepper certainly has more feeling than you do.

JENNIFER. Oh Clive, I hope we're not getting into one of our na, na, na, na, silly arguments.

CLIVE. You started it.

JENNIFER. We are.

The doorbell rings.

CLIVE. Jesus, who the hell can that be at this hour?

JENNIFER. Probably one of the video burglars. You answer it in a manly voice.

CLIVE *opens the door.*

CLIVE. Rowena.

ROWENA. Clive.

CLIVE. Good grief, we were just talking about you, weren't we, darling?

JENNIFER. Rowena, are you all right? What on earth are you doing here? Is Trevor with you?

ROWENA. I'm on my own, Mother. Nothing's wrong. Just hadn't seen you for a long time. Sorry I didn't get round to ringing back when you called. How are you both?

CLIVE (*puts his arm round* JENNIFER). We're fine, absolutely. At one. Aren't we darling?

JENNIFER (*smiling*). Ace.

ROWENA. Mum, I er, I wanted to talk to you.

JENNIFER. Oh dear, I rather think you pre-empted this conversation by giving me a copy of *My Mother Myself* last Christmas.

CLIVE. I think I'd better be making tracks. It's nice to see you Rowena. Maybe you and Trevor could come down for a weekend some time.

ROWENA. Thank you, Clive.

CLIVE. Good night all. (*He kisses* JENNIFER.)

JENNIFER. Good night, darling.

CLIVE *goes off.*

ROWENA. I feel rather silly coming this late at night.

JENNIFER. Nonsense, dear. Clive always reckons I'm less able to relax than a sex maniac dosed with Spanish Fly. Sorry, I forgot you get paid not to mock the afflicted.

ROWENA. Mother, do you have to act batty all the time?

JENNIFER. Do you want me to act bitter?

ROWENA. It was a stupid idea me coming to see you.

JENNIFER (*sits down*). Rowena, I am far too inhibited to proceed into an embarrassing mother-daughter baring of soul, but I am only half as obnoxious as I appear. What brings you here?

ROWENA. Nothing, I only wanted a chat. Have you seen anything of Mark?

JENNIFER. Unfortunately, Clive had rather an aversion to him. Ever since he wore that earring to mum's funeral. Mark, I mean, not Clive. God, Clive thinks it's cissy to carry a handkerchief. Hence he always appears more sniffy than cissy.

ROWENA. I thought Clive liked Mark.

JENNIFER. Did you? I should never have married a younger man.

ROWENA. At least I didn't make that mistake.

JENNIFER. No, you married that big dick Trevor.

ROWENA. Mother.

JENNIFER. Sorry, little prick.

They both laugh.

ROWENA. Are you and Clive happy?

Silence.

JENNIFER. No.

ROWENA. Oh? You always seem so happy to me.

JENNIFER. Why do you ask then?

Brief pause.

Since the time I married him, Clive has had numerous
affairs and what did I do? I read all the right books, I
became a perfect cook in the kitchen, perfect hostess in the
dining-room and perfect mistress in the bedroom. When that
failed, I became mistress in the bedroom, bathroom,
living-room, kitchen and lavatory.

ROWENA. Why are you telling me all this?

JENNIFER. Because you bloody well asked and because it was
part of a big fat lie which accumulated in the notion that a
facelift at forty would make me happy. When it didn't I
stopped bending over backwards, literally, for him, and
instead unleashed the acrimonious recriminations which
I'd kept bottled up for years.

ROWENA. I'm sorry, I never knew.

JENNIFER. I don't want your pity. I've given as good as I've
got, well, nearly. If I kill him I'll rot in prison as an evil
scheming bitch. If he kills me he'll get a suspended sentence
because I was neurotic and nagged. We are always responsible
for their crimes but we carry the can for our own.

ROWENA. Does he still have affairs?

JENNIFER. He tries but he can't fulfil the false image in his
head of how a woman should behave.

ROWENA. Because women's sexual identity has been
manufactured.

JENNIFER. Perhaps you should write an article in *Community
Care*.

ROWENA. Do you remember that night we went out to dinner?

JENNIFER. How could I forget?

ROWENA. Did you think Yvonne made sense?

JENNIFER. Oh yes.

ROWENA. Why didn't you back her up?

JENNIFER. I wasn't aware it was a debate. Next time I'll round
up a chief whip. Look, darling, it's no good putting your head
in the sand and crying about it.

ROWENA. Why not?

JENNIFER. For one thing you get grit in your eyelids. (*Pause*.)
Sorry. (*She sighs*.) It's late. I'd better switch the electric
blanket on in the spare bed. I take it you're staying, course
you are. I've forgotten whether you're a breakfast person or
not.

ROWENA. I don't think you ever knew.

JENNIFER. Huh, many's the time I can remember mediating
between you and Mark over who had the most Rice Crispies.
It was practically bloody lunchtime before you two actually
got round to eating them after listening to them going snap
crackle and pop for hours. Anyway, you'll have to make
do with toast.

Pause.

I never really liked being a mother much. I'd always looked
forward to the time when we could be friends. (*Slight pause*.)
God knows, the company round here is awful. (*Picks up the
video*.)

ROWENA (*takes the video from* JENNIFER). Is that what you
do? Watch these things with him?

JENNIFER. I used to but not any more. If they did to dogs what
they do to women on the screen, there'd be a public uproar.

ROWENA. But he still buys them.

JENNIFER. I did once dump the lot in a bucket of water, but
not unpredictably he took violent exception to the event.

ROWENA. Not surprising.

JENNIFER. Do you know how much they cost?

ROWENA. Tough.

Scene Twelve

TREVOR *is putting the finishing touches to the table*. YVONNE *and* RON *are coming to dinner. The sound of a door slamming*.

TREVOR. Not a moment too soon, love, look. (*He gestures towards the table*.) All my own work. They'll be here any minute. Oh no, what's up? This evening visiting is getting a real bind. Don't tell me, Hilary's murdered Heathcliffe and hidden him in a cupboard.

ROWENA. She's left the job.

TREVOR. I'll restrain myself from saying I told you so.

ROWENA. Fucking hell.

TREVOR. Suppose it was quite ungrateful of her.

ROWENA. There's a limit to gratitude.

TREVOR. I know sometimes it's really tedious when people don't behave according to plan.

ROWENA. Ron has been offering her lifts home and automatically assumed he could sleep with her.

TREVOR. She shouldn't have accepted the lifts then, she's not as innocent as that.

ROWENA (*sarcastic*). It's that simple, that clear cut, isn't it?

TREVOR. It's not as if she's averse to sleeping with men for gain.

ROWENA. Oh fuck off.

TREVOR. Look, you know things aren't good mutually — and I used the word advisedly — between him and Yvonne, so he has a bit on the side.

ROWENA (*louder*). A bit on the side?! So it could be anyone — he has a universal right . . .

TREVOR. She only had to say no — like you do, often enough. If matricide means beating the mattress to death we can both plead not guilty with a free conscience.

ROWENA. Don't you understand at all why I'm so angry?

TREVOR. Why take it out on me? I haven't done anything.

ROWENA. Except condone the idea that half the human race are mere objects with suitable orifices.

TREVOR. Don't be totally ridiculous.

The doorbell rings.

ROWENA. Don't answer it.

TREVOR. For God's sake, stop acting like a petulant child. She's your friend, make a bloody effort. (*He opens the door. Very politely.*) Hello Ron, Yvonne, how nice to see you . . . come in . . . Row's just got in from work . . . I don't know if you want to change, darling.

ROWENA. What into — a mute frog?

RON. Oh there's no need, you look perfectly lovely, Row.

TREVOR. Row? Drink everyone? (*He pours them all a glass of wine.*) There you go . . . umm, well . . . Row?

ROWENA. Just adjusting the *bonhommie* to automatic pilot. How are you Yvonne?

TREVOR (*to* RON). Can't seem to get her out of jeans these days.

YVONNE. The same. I've written to publishing firms about another job.

ROWENA. Good.

TREVOR. Shall we take a pew before the avocados shrivel before our eyes? Yvonne? Ron? (*He gestures towards the table. They sit.*)

ROWENA. Time for the last supper.

ROWENA *sits.*

RON. This all looks very good. There was really no need you know. That girl was a good worker but I suppose you know she up and left.

ROWENA. Yes.

RON. It was the hours.

ROWENA. I heard.

RON. It was nice to have her about the place — bright spark.

ROWENA. I'm sure.

RON. I'd be willing to give her another chance.

ROWENA. How chivalrous of you.

RON. Don't worry, it won't prejudice me against anyone else you might put my way.

ROWENA (*deliberately drops a knife on her plate, pause*). You've got a nerve.

RON. A charm, a certain brash charm.

YVONNE. Charm? Charm, my arm.

RON. No need for pleasantries, love.

ROWENA (*to* RON). How dare you rape that woman.

RON. That's no woman, that's my wife.

ROWENA. Hilary, one of my clients.

RON. Don't be so possessive. I was one of her clients, and do you mind, there was no force involved.

ROWENA. No fucking choice involved.

TREVOR. Rowena, you're giving fucking a bad name.

RON. Look, I did her a favour, I gave her a job don't forget.

ROWENA. I'm not about to, nor is she.

RON. At least she's now got some work experience.

ROWENA. I don't believe this.

RON. And of course I'd be prepared to give her a reference.

ROWENA. Oh, I'm sure, I'm sure.

RON. So, right? There's no need to take on, okay.

ROWENA. You bastard.

TREVOR (*still trying to save the situation*). Now you're taking the name of the illegitimate in vain.

The following lines, up to RON's *and* TREVOR's *exit, are all delivered at top speed and volume.*

ROWENA. Get stuffed.

TREVOR. Just shut it, will you?

YVONNE. Why should she?

RON. You stay out of this.

ROWENA. Why should she?

TREVOR. Just leave it.

YVONNE. Oh, you'd like that wouldn't you?

RON. Who told you to open your trap?

TREVOR. For Chrissakes, drop it.

YVONNE (*to* RON). Who gave you the right to breathe?

RON. Shut it before I shut it for you.

ROWENA. Get out of my sight. Get out of my house.

TREVOR. Leaving aside the theory, all property is theft. It's our house.

YVONNE. Clever Trevor.

ROWENA. Shut up Trevor.

TREVOR (*to* YVONNE). You make me sick.

YVONNE. The feeling's mutual.

RON. Just bloody well piss off.

ROWENA. No, you piss off yourself.

TREVOR. Shut up.

YVONNE. No, you shut up.

TREVOR. You stupid bitch.

RON (*to* ROWENA *and* YVONNE). You make me ill — the pair of you.

YVONNE (*screams*). Then get out.

RON. Don't worry. I won't spend another moment with you — you fucking hysterical hag.

YVONNE. The truth, the elusive truth, slipped inadvertently from the pig's mouth.

RON. I'm off. (*He goes out.*) Witch.

TREVOR. Ron wait for me. (*He goes out.*)

   Long pause.

ROWENA. Ah, well, Trevor never makes enough for four.

YVONNE. I'm not very hungry.

ROWENA. What are you going to do?

YVONNE. Leave him.

Scene Thirteen

A cold but sunny spring day. ROWENA, YVONNE *and* JENNIFER *are having a picnic. The atmosphere between them is warm and relaxed. The pace is slow.*

JENNIFER. I don't think I've been on a picnic since you were little.

ROWENA. I must confess it wasn't a habit I thought I'd be keeping up.

YVONNE. It's nice though . . . reminds me of when I was a kid . . . rolling down grass slopes in the park . . .

ROWENA. Trying to fend off the wasps from the jam sandwiches . . .

YVONNE. Playing run outs . . .

ROWENA. Playing on the swings in the park till after dark.

JENNIFER. When the only thing you had to worry about was forgetting your dinner money for school.

YVONNE. I didn't even have to worry about that. I used to get free school dinners.

ROWENA. And I had packed lunches and (*To* JENNIFER:) you used to throw anything in them that just happened to be in the fridge at the time . . .

YVONNE. Which, as far as I remember, was usually beetroot . . .

ROWENA. That's right, we used to share my packed lunches, and your dinner tickets and have two dinners together a week . . .

YVONNE. And sell off the extra one and spend the money in the tuck shop on Fridays.

JENNIFER. I see . . . It's all coming out now . . . Did you ever sell off the packed lunches?

ROWENA. You must be joking. We'd have had to pay someone to eat beetroot sandwiches.

All laugh. Then silence.

JENNIFER. I always used to loathe the spring . . .

YVONNE. Seems one of the most unlikely things to loathe.

JENNIFER. All that stuff about everything new . . . growing . . . new start and all that only served to make me want to squash it all.

ROWENA. You've never allowed yourself to be optimistic . . .

JENNIFER. I think it was more the awful feeling of being left behind. (*Pause.*) Still, at last I'm starting to blossom. I've become more adventurous in my old age.

YVONNE. You've got the Family Planning Association to sponsor a flower arranging exhibition?

JENNIFER. No, that was a load of rubbish . . . I'm going on holiday to Greece. How's that for starters?

ROWENA. Nice. Are you going on your own?

JENNIFER. Originally yes, but I wondered if you two wanted to come with me . . .

YVONNE. That sounds like a great idea . . .

ROWENA. Hang on, we can't even afford . . .

JENNIFER. On me I meant. It's the least I can do to make up for the beetroot sandwiches.

ROWENA. When?

JENNIFER. Easter?

ROWENA (*to* YVONNE). What do you think?

YVONNE. I'd love it.

JENNIFER. Right, that's settled then.

Silence.

ROWENA. Well, I suppose we better start making a move . . . get all this packed up.

YVONNE. I sort of wish we didn't have to go back . . .

JENNIFER. If we stay here much longer we won't have to, we'll die from exposure . . .

YVONNE. Shame the sun had to go in.

JENNIFER. The sun never goes in. It just gets obscured by clouds.

ROWENA. Very poetic, Mother.

JENNIFER. See, how's that for optimism?

Scene Fourteen

Tube station. It is 10.30 p.m. A man enters. There is the sound of a train pulling in. He sits on a bench, half-asleep, free to doze. ROWENA rushes on to the platform. As the train pulls out another man enters smoking a cigarette. There is the sound off of a tube approaching on another platform. The man looks at his watch. Pause. He casually saunters up the platform towards ROWENA who doesn't look at him. Long pause. He then says something to her which we don't hear. She turns away and weighs up the options of whether to run back up an empty, dark passageway or stay where she is. She moves away from him deciding that the next train will arrive any minute and she'll be safe. He approaches her again very fast. Very close to her face. She shoves him violently. He falls on the track. There is the sound of a train. Simultaneous blackout. Lights flash on ROWENA looking back at the track. Blackout. The train screeches to a halt.

Scene Fifteen

Music: the tune from Scene Eight. A POLICEWOMAN *stands in the shadow behind* ROWENA. *There is the sound of a knock at the door and then front door opening. All dialogue to the end of the scene is pre-recorded.*

ROWENA. Hello Hilary I . . .

HILARY. Go to hell.

ROWENA (*firmly*). Hang on. (*Then:*) The nursery rang to say that Heathcliffe hasn't been for the last couple of days. Is he all right?

HILARY. He's okay so you can stop concerning yourself.

ROWENA. Then why hasn't he . . . ?

HILARY (*very aggressive*). Cos I ain't bin well.

ROWENA (*relieved*). Oh, I see. (*Then:*) Have you been off work?

HILARY. You're quick.

ROWENA. Don't worry, I'm sure Ron will understand.

HILARY. I'm sure he does.

ROWENA. Luckily he and his wife are coming round to dinner this evening. I'll explain . . .

HILARY. Save yerself the trouble. I've told him to stuff his job.

ROWENA (*pause*). Well . . . sure . . . if that's your choice.

HILARY (*shouts*). Just what's it to you anyway? Nothing. All you bloody care about is Heathcliffe. You don't give a bleedin' monkeys about me.

ROWENA. Look, can I come in . . . ?

HILARY. No, you can fuck off.

ROWENA. Hilary . . .

HILARY. I wish to God I'd never set eyes on you — you and your bleedin' friends.

ROWENA. He did give you a job.

HILARY. Yeah, oh yeah, and I'll give you three guesses what he expected in return an' all.

ROWENA. What?

HILARY. What d'you think? Use yer imagination.

ROWENA. The bastard! Hilary I'm sorry . . .

HILARY. And that's about all you can afford to be an' all.
'Sorry'. 'Cos you ain't ever going to know what it's like to be
thrown on the shit heap. You got enough qualifications,
security and money to have some sodding choice. Well mine
is the D bloody HSS crap. Or on me back. What a bloody joke
and I thought working was s'posed to give you some
self-respect. Ha bloody ha.

ROWENA (*angry rather than lost for words*). God, I don't know
what to say.

HILARY. Why bother to say anything? You just have your nice
dinner party, smooth everything over and live happily ever
after.

The sound of the front door slamming.

Scene Sixteen

Courtroom. JUDGE, COUNSEL FOR THE PROSECUTION.

JUDGE. Mrs Stone. Mrs Stone. (ROWENA *faces the* JUDGE.)
We have heard the evidence, including extensive psychiatric
reports which suggest you are removed, vague, uninvolved,
and failed to maintain normal, acceptable patterns of
communication. Prudish to the point of being sexually
repressed — frigid. Is there anything you would like to say?

ROWENA. Yes. (*She reads from a piece of paper.*) Douglas
Coles pleaded guilty to the manslaughter of his wife and
got two years' probation because it was proved she was
neurotic and nagged. Gordon Asher strangled his wife and got
a six-month suspended sentence. (*In future productions more
up-to-date examples can be substituted for these.*)

JUDGE. Please don't waste this court's valuable time with

irrelevant material. You have chosen to present your own
defence. I suggest you do so by re-examining in your own
words the events leading up to the crime.

ROWENA (*pause*). He spoke to me.

PROSECUTION. I am speaking to you. Do you mean to say that
if I were standing in a tube station I might meet my end?

ROWENA *does not respond.*

What did he say to you?

ROWENA. I don't remember.

PROSECUTION. You don't remember? (*He speaks louder.*) Do
you remember the crime? The consequences? The punishment
for a few words exchanged?

Silence.

JUDGE. Please try to elaborate a little, Mrs Stone.

ROWENA. I'd been to see a film, a pornographic film. I was
extremely angry.

JUDGE. You are not at liberty to avenge the pornography
industry in this country. We have censorship laws for that.

ROWENA. The laws are a load of cock.

PROSECUTION. Mrs Stone, I really must . . .

JUDGE. Indeed, the laws will need looking into if they provoke
this callous sort of attack from so-called sane women. What
was this film?

ROWENA. A snuff movie.

PROSECUTION (*in response to* JUDGE*'s puzzled look*). M'lud,
a film or films made in the United States where, according to
reliable reports, the participant is actually killed in front of
the camera.

JUDGE. What, in real life?

PROSECUTION. Yes, m'lud.

JUDGE. So, on seeing this film you thought you'd go out and
kill a man?

ROWENA. No, it was a coincidence. I didn't want to speak to that man. He insisted, when he got too close for comfort I became angry and shoved him.

PROSECUTION. Unfortunately, on to the line, at the time when the train was coming. Why didn't you shove him back on to the platform?

ROWENA. I . . .

PROSECUTION. Because this was an act committed in cold blood, regardless of the accused's inexplicable preamble . . . Watching a film cannot be construed as anything but an objective experience. The man was a complete stranger and there is no foreseeable way that it could be described as a crime of passion. He leaves a wife who would not be a widow today if it had not been for the calculated acts of this woman.

ROWENA. What was he doing harassing me then?

PROSECUTION. Harassing you? You can't even remember what he said. 'Have you got a light?', or 'Can you tell me the time?' Are you seriously suggesting that innocent remarks should be deemed incitement to murder?

JUDGE. Mrs Stone we have heard the evidence. One thing is indisputable. A man has lost his life as the direct consequence of the action taken against him by you. A man whom you have admitted you never met before. I would suggest to you that the evidence you have put forward is nothing more than an irrelevant fabrication to further some fanatical belief that the laws concerning pornography in this country are inadequate. But that is of no concern here.

He looks at her. She looks directly back at him.

Do you understand, Mrs Stone, that it is now up to this court to determine whether you are guilty or not guilty?

Silence.

CLERK (*voice over*). All stand.

ROWENA *and the* POLICEWOMAN *move forward into an 'empty' room. The* POLICEWOMAN *sits on a bench.*

Scene Seventeen

ROWENA *and* POLICEWOMAN. ROWENA *is absorbed in her own thoughts. There is silence.*

POLICEWOMAN. Is there anything I can get for you . . . ?

ROWENA. What? Oh. No . . . Thanks.

POLICEWOMAN. Cigarette. (*She offers her one.*) What was it like?

ROWENA. Sorry?

POLICEWOMAN. The film you saw.

ROWENA. Oh, that.

POLICEWOMAN. What was it like? Er, don't . . . If you don't want to.

Pause.

ROWENA (*very quietly*). Well, the first part was badly made and like a lot of films it contained a good deal of violence and shooting. I think it was loosely based on the Charles Manson story. Then it changes, it becomes real. It's a film studio during a break in the filming. The director is near a bed talking to a young woman. He gets turned on and wants to have sex with her. They lie on the bed and he kisses her. She then realises that they are being filmed. She doesn't like it and protests. There is a knife lying on the bed near her shoulder. He pins her down as she attempts to get up. He picks up the knife and moves it round her neck and throat. There is utter terror on her face as she realises that he is not acting. She tries to get up but cannot. The film shows shots of his face which registers power and pleasure. He starts to cut into her shoulder, and the pain in her face . . . It's real . . . Blood seeps through her blouse. Her arm is held down and he cuts off her fingers. It is terrible. I have watched a woman being cut up and she is alive. He then picks up an electric saw. And I think no . . . no he can't use it. But he does. Her hand is sawn off . . . left twitching by her side. Then he plunges the saw into her stomach, and the pain and terror on her face. More shots of his face of power and pleasure. He puts his hands inside her and pulls out some of her insides. Finally, he reaches in again and pulls out her guts and holds them above his head. He is triumphant.

Long pause.

That's it. The end. And I kept forcing myself, to pretend that it was only a movie.

POLICEWOMAN. No. It happens. I've seen photos, hundreds of photos of little girls, young women, middle-aged women, old women . . . with torn genitals, ripped vaginas, mutilated beyond recognition. I try to not think about it.

ROWENA. I'm going to have a long time to think about it.

POLICEWOMAN. We do our best to convict them.

ROWENA. Yes. (ROWENA *moves away*.) I don't want anything to do with men who have knives or whips or men who look at photos of women tied and bound, or men who say relax and enjoy it. Or men who tell misogynist jokes.

Blackout.